THE PAWNEE

ARTHUR MYERS

THE PAWNEE

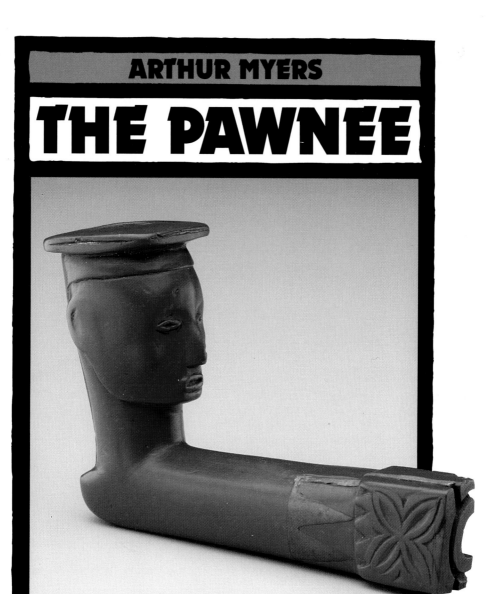

Franklin Watts   *New York*   *Chicago*   *London*   *Sydney*   *A First Book*

Map by Joe LeMonnier

Photographs copyright ©: cover: Jim Argo; 3: Detroit Institute of Arts, Founders
Society Purchase; 12: Historical Pictures/Stock Montage; 16, 20: The Kansas State
Historical Society, Topeka; 18: Buffalo Bill Historical Center, Cody, Wyoming, gift
of William E. Weiss; 22: National Museum of the American Indian; 23, 52, 53, 54,
55 (both), 56, 57: Jim Argo; 24, 29: National Museum of American Art,
Washington, DC/Art Resource, New York; 26 (both), 37, 40, 44: Ayer Collection,
The Newberry Library; 33, 35, 50: John Running; 43: University of Michigan
Museum of Art, Bequest of Henry C. Lewis; 46: UPI/Bettmann; 47: Archives &
Manuscripts Division, Oklahoma Hisorical Society; 48: Western History
Collections, University of Oklahoma Library

Library of Congress Cataloging-in-Publication Data

Myers, Arthur.
The Pawnee / by Arthur Myers.
p. cm. — (A First book)
Includes bibliographical references (p.) and index.
Summary: Discusses the traditional and modern way of life of the Pawnee,
examining their culture, religion, and codes of conduct.
ISBN 0-531-20165-1 (lib. bdg.)
1. Pawnee Indians—Juvenile literature. [1. Pawnee Indians. 2. Indians of North
America—Great Plains.] I. Title. II. Series.
E99.P3M97 1993
978.2'004975—dc20   93-18369 CIP AC

CONTENTS

To Cima Star

THE PAWNEE

A TALE OF TRIAL AND DEATH AND SLAVERY

The Pawnee are a tribe with a history of perhaps even more bad luck than was usual among North American Indian tribes after the coming of the Europeans. They gained fame in the nineteenth century as Pawnee Scouts, serving as guides for and fighting with U.S. army forces against other Indian tribes. Yet they were feared and hated by westward-bound settlers who streamed through Pawnee country. The settlers overwhelmed the Pawnee, intruding on their land, killing buffalo, and disrupting the Pawnees' way of life. In defense, the Pawnee sometimes struck back at wagon trains and settlements.

The Pawnee take pride in having never fought a war with the United States—that is, with the white man. Yet the U.S. government treated the Pawnee

THIS ENGRAVING FROM ABOUT 1858 SHOWS A PAWNEE MAN
LOOKING OUT FOR ATTACKERS FROM AN ENEMY TRIBE.

worse than tribes such as the Sioux or Apache, who fought bitterly against the white man and his armed forces. The politicians in Washington, D.C., most likely saw the Pawnee as easy to push around and thus gave them fewer weapons, metal implements, gifts, and other support than they gave more aggressive tribes.

Before the coming of white settlers to the Pawnees' home in what is now Nebraska, the tribe numbered about ten thousand. By the early years of the twentieth century, the Pawnees' numbers had shrunk to approximately 600. They became almost a memory. This was not only because of devastating battles with other tribes, but because of diseases brought by the settlers, to which the Indians had little or no immunity. In 1831, an epidemic of smallpox killed nearly half the Pawnee, and in 1849 cholera swept away another 1,200 people. The Pawnee were raided constantly by the Sioux; drought and grasshoppers destroyed their crops; and the buffalo, killed in gigantic numbers by the white man for sport, became ever more scarce.

The Pawnee are part of a large grouping of Indians called the *Caddo*, a word that means "children of the earth." The Caddoan-speaking people are believed to have come from what is now Mexico, but they moved northward and by the 1600s were in

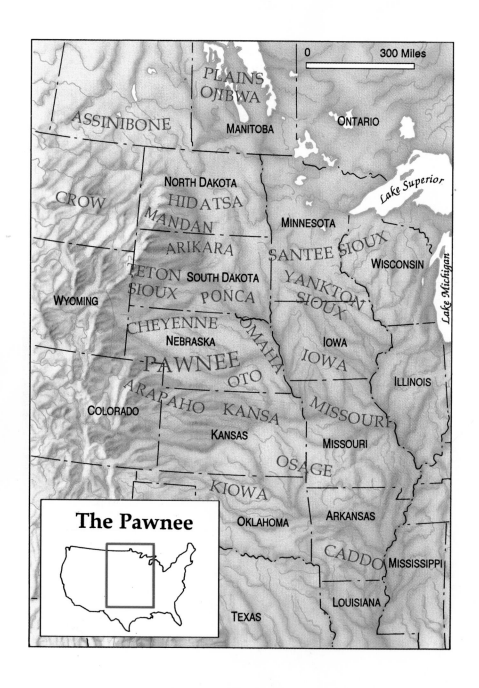

The Pawnee

control of large areas of the Western plains. During this time period they were the dominant people of that region, pushing the Plains Apache and Dakota Sioux northward before them. This was the Golden Age of the Pawnee.

The origin of the name *Pawnee* has various explanations. Some say it comes from the Caddoan word *pariki*, which means horn, because Pawnee men wore their hair so heavily plastered with grease and paint that it stood erect like an animal's horn. Other historians say the name came from a Sioux word that means feathers because the Pawnee were fond of using bright feathers in their clothing and religious ceremonies. And some say the name comes from another Caddoan word *parisu*, meaning hunter.

The Pawnees, although they could be aggressive fighters, tended to be a peaceful, agricultural tribe. They had what at first seemed good fortune in that their homelands were comparatively distant from the white man, with other tribes serving as buffers. This situation eventually became a disadvantage for the Pawnees because they were last in line to receive what the white man had to offer, both good and bad. These included metal implements such as knives, which could be used in both peaceful and warlike pursuits; textiles that could be used for clothing; and, perhaps most significantly, horses and firearms.

THE MASS SLAUGHTER OF THE BUFFALO BY SETTLERS CHANGED
THE WAY OF LIFE FOR THE PAWNEE.

Unfortunately for the Pawnee, neighboring tribes such as the Sioux, the Comanche, and the Apache were exposed to these questionable benefits of the white man decades before the Pawnee. Armed only with stone and flint weapons and fighting on foot, the Pawnee were at a disastrous disadvantage to other tribes who had horses and guns. Village after Pawnee village was slaughtered and enslaved by tribes that possessed these new weapons of battle. There were so many Pawnee slaves that at one time the word Pawnee came to mean slave, even though many Indian slaves were not Pawnees.

"SURROUND OF BUFFALO BY INDIANS"
BY ALFRED JACOB MILLER

LIFE IN A PAWNEE VILLAGE

Most of the Indian tribes of the Western plains were *nomadic*. They moved constantly, following the wandering buffalo, their chief supply of food and hides. Their homes were cone-shaped *tipis* made of animal skin, easily dismantled and taken along on their travels. The Pawnee, however, tended to live in more permanent villages. Their homes were solid earthen huts, circular in shape and made from soil and timber.

The Pawnee were basically an agricultural people rather than hunters, but in the early 1700s, when the Pawnee came into possession of horses and guns, hunting buffalo became more important in their lives. Because they were becoming more nomadic, they added tipis to their means of shelter, so they needed animal hides.

A PAWNEE ENCAMPMENT IN THE
PLATTE RIVER VALLEY IN NEBRASKA

During the summer, especially if crops were not good, the tribe would take to the plains and seek buffalo, hoping for a quick kill and food. If the hunt was successful, great hunks of meat would be roasted or baked, and the hungry people would gorge themselves. After a spree of eating, more buffalo would be slaughtered for hides and food for the winter. Many of the poorer hides would be shaved to make rawhide boxes. Heavier hides were used for tipis or winter coats.

Fowl such as quail and prairie chickens were often hunted for food, usually by boys using long poles. Small animals such as raccoons, otter, and skunks were sometimes killed for food, but mainly for their skins, which could be used in moccasins and for other clothing items. At times, the Pawnee traded in furs with the French and Spanish.

Pawnee villages were likely to be found in the comfort of wooded river valleys, protected from the harsh winds of the open plains. There, the people could cultivate crops and collect firewood for cooking, heating, making pottery, and drying corn. Wood was also used for tipi poles and for earth lodges.

The Pawnee planted a variety of crops. These included ten to fifteen kinds of corn, seven kinds of pumpkins and squash, and eight kinds of beans. Watermelons and sunflowers were also raised. The plots of land were assigned by the village chief, and people were entitled to these fields year after year. The best land was found in creek bottoms, near natural springs and near the mouths of ravines. Sometimes the women had to go 7 or 8 miles (11–13 km) from the village to get to the choicest fields.

AN EXAMPLE OF A PAWNEE PAINTED PARFLECHE
(BAG OR CASE MADE OF RAW HIDE)

THESE MOCCASINS ARE A FINE EXAMPLE OF THE INTRICATE
BEADING THAT EXISTED ON MUCH OF THE PAWNEE'S CLOTHING.

"YOUNG OMAHAW, WAR EAGLE, LITTLE MISSOURI AND
PAWNEES," A 1821 PAINTING BY CHARLES BIRD KING

While the women did the work of cultivating the soil, the Pawnee men attended to other matters, such as hunting and conducting political and religious activities. They tended to divide much of physical labor beneath them. One white missionary of the mid-nineteenth century said, "The [Pawnee] women perform more hard labor than any women I have ever seen . . . while the men eat, smoke, sleep, sing, gamble, go to war and steal horses." Other observers, however, noted that the women did not find their work degrading, and in fact were proud and enthusiastic about it. Pawnee men sometimes helped with the farming, but when they did, it was more in the spirit of fun than serious, steady work.

During the nineteenth century, the conquering whites tried to turn the Indians' life into an imitation of white society. But many whites, and certainly many Indians, did not agree with this way of thinking. A modern historian and anthropologist, Gene Weltfish, writes in her book, *The Lost Universe*, "The basic Pawnee household was as different from ours as it is possible for a human arrangement to be. And yet it gave personal satisfaction to its members."

The Pawnee community was composed of a village of about a dozen, sometimes several dozen, earth *lodges*—large dome-shaped buildings housing twenty to fifty people each, the occupants sometimes chang-

ABOVE, THIS HISTORIC PHOTO SHOWS THE EARTH LODGES FOR WHICH THE PAWNEE ARE FAMOUS; LEFT, ANOTHER VIEW OF THE PAWNEE EARTH LODGES WITH A FAMILY POSING IN FRONT.

ing from season to season. Pawnee men often had more than one wife, and the women often had more than one husband. The children considered themselves all brothers and sisters.

The Pawnee people were quite unlike the popular idea of Plains Indians such as the Cheyenne and Sioux, who were hunters moving from place to place and, living by war. The Pawnee, rather, tended to be sedentary, staying in one place. They were more interested in agriculture, religion, and arts such as dancing than were their more warring neighbors. Yet that could have been a reason for their decline. The primary interest of Pawnee society was not power and aggression, but peaceful pursuits and living together in harmony.

Also, living in permanent villages, they were easy targets. The wandering tribes of the Plains always knew where the Pawnee would be, and that they would probably be off their guard. Their houses were spread out. Such villages have been called death traps. They were more difficult to defend than the constantly moving, closely gathered tipis of other Plains Indians. The nomadic Sioux murdered Pawnee women in the fields, burned and trampled their corn, and robbed their food *caches*. The Pawnee men returned from hunts to find their earth lodges destroyed and old people who had remained behind dead. Sometimes in desperation, the Pawnees threatened to abandon the villages forever and become nomads themselves, yet they never did. But such continuous attacks, as well as deadly epidemics, drained much of the Pawnees' offensive spirit. Pawnee heroes of history were usually men who died fighting to defend their women and children.

The Pawnee were not the sort of people to take orders easily from authority. Their society did not operate along rigid, dictatorial lines. Rather than being organized warriors, they became expert horse rustlers. They preferred to deal with their enemies in this manner, which required less aggression and discipline than war. A Pawnee expedition usually involved a party of braves traveling across hundreds of miles of plains into the enemies' territory, stealthily approaching an enemy camp, and sweeping off herds of horses in the night.

The Pawnees had hereditary chiefs, meaning that sons of chiefs followed their fathers into chiefdom. Although a man was born to this status, he had to exhibit suitable knowledge and behavior to wield power. One historian, Preston Holder, describes the Pawnee leaders as "men to whom violence was a stranger. Their voices were never raised in anger or threatened violence. Their image was one of large knowledge, quiet patience, and thorough understanding."

"HORSE CHIEF, GRAND PAWNEE HEAD CHIEF"
PAINTED BY GEORGE CATLIN IN 1834.

The Pawnee had discipline, but the discipline came from within each person. Commands were not issued. Assignments for work were not made. Codes of conduct were not emphasized. People did what they felt should be done. This sense of democratic self-reliance developed from earliest childhood, when each child was treated as a dignified, independent person.

In the Pawnee village, there was little of the sharp difference in the amount of possessions that is found in most societies. The sharing of goods began with the family. It flowed upward to the chiefs and priests, but most of the wealth paused only briefly at the top. Then it was given back, and the others in the village shared in it.

Although the chiefs and priests were men, family life was dominated by women. The most important person in each family and lodge was the oldest woman. The father was only considered to have married into the family. And here, in the lodges, was the real center of Pawnee village life.

THE SPIRITUAL LIFE OF THE PAWNEE

The Pawnee took a deep interest in the spirit, in the forces that might lie behind the physical life. They believed in a supreme being, called *Tirawa*, or The One Above. From Tirawa, they believed, came all things, including the heavens and the stars. The chief stars in the religious thought of the Pawnee were the Evening Star, which symbolized woman, and the Morning Star, symbolic of man. The Pawnee religion taught that the Morning Star had gone forth to seek the Evening Star, so that creation might be achieved.

Priests, sometimes called medicine men, were very important in the life of the Pawnee. These men, whom the Pawnee saw as messengers between the unseen spirit world and the ordinary world, presided when seeds were planted. They watched the skies during the growing season. They performed ceremonies to drive away storms and resist other dangers to crops. They used magical rites to seek success in buffalo hunts and in other activities of the village. They used herbs and charms to combat illnesses. The priests ruled over medicine lodges filled with stuffed birds and animals, which were objects used in religious ceremonies.

The symbolic soul of the Pawnees' spiritual life was their sacred bundles. Each lodge had its own bundle, as did each village, each dancing society, and each warrior. The most powerful bundles were held by the chiefs, but they were used only by priests.

A typical bundle was described by a historian as containing "a buffalo robe, fancifully dressed, skins of several fur bearing animals, the skull of a wild cat, stuffed skins of a sparrow hawk, several bundles of scalps and broken arrows taken from enemies, a small bundle of Pawnee arrows, some ears of corn and a few wads of buffalo hair." A bundle of this sort was believed to contain great power.

The Pawnee were regarded by other Indian tribes as mystery men, with the status of gods or superhumans. Other tribes were awed by the Pawnees' rituals and their poetic interpretations of the heavens and the earth. The Indians of New Mexico once told the famed Spanish explorer, Coronado, that great men

THE RICH PAWNEE TRADITION OF FESTIVALS AND
CEREMONIES CONTINUES TODAY.

lived to the north. He hastened to see them, but the Pawnees struck him as nothing more than half-naked Indians whose speech he could not understand. He was so angry that he killed his Indian guide. To Coronado, greatness meant gold; to the guide, it had meant grandeur and beauty of thought.

The Pawnee had many festivals. The harvest festival was held in the fall and lasted for twenty nights. Ceremonies began at midnight, when the constellation of stars today called the Pleiades was directly overhead. The Pawnee believed that these seven stars had been set in the heavens to form a guide to their tribe, so that its people would not become lost.

The fall festival was full of chanting, music, and performances by clowns and magicians. It was called by the Pawnees the "Big-Sleight-of-Hand." The whites called it "The Opera." Many white witnesses have testified that the feats performed were amazing. Bears and other savage animals would appear suddenly in the big medicine lodge where the performances were held. The animals pursued and mangled the people; then the medicine men cured what seemed to be fatal wounds. Men were shot or stabbed and seemed to fall dead, only to be revived quickly and cured. Seeds such as maize were planted, sprouted, and reached full growth within minutes, under the watchful eyes of wondering Indians and white men.

CHANTING AND MUSIC ARE AT THE
CENTER OF MANY PAWNEE FESTIVALS.

One group of the Pawnee, the *Skidi*, up until the early nineteenth century, had a custom that many outsiders found repellent. This ritual required the sacrifice of a young girl to the Morning Star. Pawnee warriors would attack the camp of another tribe killing and scalping people, but sparing an adolescent girl. They would carry her to their home. There she was accorded great respect and beautifully dressed. On the day of the sacrifice, her body was painted red on the right side and black on the left. The red symbolized day, the time of the Morning Star; the black represented night, the time of the Evening Star. After elaborate ceremonies, the girl was led to a scaffold and told to climb it. Her hands and feet were bound. She was shot through the heart by an arrow. Then a priest rushed upon her, cut out her heart, and offered it to the Morning Star.

By the 1820s, white society had considerable contact with the Pawnee and disapproved strongly of this ceremony. The important chiefs of the tribe were beginning to realize that they would have to abide by the wishes of this powerful people. One young chief, Man Chief, or *Pita-rusaru*, was convinced this ceremony must not continue. One day, when the girl had been tied to the scaffold and a warrior was prepared to shoot the fatal arrow, Man Chief rode before the assemblage and said he had come to rescue the girl or

MAN CHIEF MADE AN IMPORTANT CHANGE IN PAWNEE
TRADITION AND RITUAL BY ENDING THE PRACTICE OF
SACRIFICING A YOUNG MAIDEN TO THE MORNING STAR.

die in the attempt. By tribal belief, anyone who touched the girl would soon die, for he would be taken by the Morning Star in her place. But Man Chief defied this belief. As the crowd stood in awe, he cut the girl down, placed her on a horse, and took her back safely to the village of her people.

Soon after, Man Chief went to Washington, D.C., with a delegation of chiefs. A group of white women presented him with a large silver medal on which was inscribed: *"To the Bravest of the Brave."*

THE WITHERING OF THE WORLD OF THE PAWNEE

In the early 1800s, the white man began to move westward in earnest. The famed explorers Meriwether Lewis and William Clark met the Pawnee and called them "a fine-looking people." Another white visitor, Major George Sibley, called them "a sober-minded and well-disposed people," but he made a remark that foreshadowed disaster to their traditional life. "There can be no true civilization without Christianity," he said.

The Pawnee were not convinced that the white man had found the key to happiness, but during the next century they were gradually forced to imitate white men. *Missionaries* moved in to coax, or compel, Indians to adopt the whites' religion. The U.S. government made efforts to prevent tribes from warring

DURING THE NINETEENTH CENTURY INDIAN CHILDREN WERE SENT TO
GOVERNMENT AND PRIVATE SCHOOLS WHERE THEY WERE FORCED TO
LEARN THE LANGUAGE AND CULTURE OF THE LARGER SOCIETY.

with each other. The Pawnees were restrained from one of their favorite traditions, plundering horses. They and other tribes were pressed to give up the hunting life and become farmers. The Pawnee had an agricultural background, but the whites insisted that the farming be done their way, not the Pawnee way. The Pawnees were discouraged from building their earthen lodges; the white man wanted them to live in wooden houses, as white Americans did. Pawnee children were gathered into schools where they were often forbidden to speak their own language. They were forced, sometimes brutally, to speak English.

Some of the whites were understanding and helpful. Others were cruel and corrupt. Some were seeking power or profit; others were simply determined to enforce their beliefs on the Indians. An example of the last was a missionary named James Mathers, who settled among the Pawnee in 1842. He tried to impose his faith with his fists and a bull whip. The Pawnee did not strike back, for they had been taught for centuries that holy men were sacred, even Christian holy men. Mathers was joined by other whites who saw nothing wrong with using the whip on the Pawnees.

The Pawnee had been driven to the brink of starvation by the Sioux and Dakota raids. Thus Pawnees began to take food from the whites' fields. If caught, they were beaten unmercifully, sometimes to the point of being permanently lamed or driven insane. One day an Indian boy was shot by Mathers' son, Carolan. This brought matters to a violent head. Soldier Chief, a Pawnee leader, went to Mathers' house to protest. A brawl broke out, and Mathers seized an ax and chopped off the chief's arm. But the Indian was not through. He grasped Mathers and threw him to the ground. Another son of Mathers, Marcellus, entered the fight, and the enraged chief tackled both father and son. Marcellus turned and fled, but Soldier Chief picked up Mathers' ax and threw it after the fleeing young man. It sank deep into Marcellus' back. Soldier Chief then died from his wound, and Marcellus died soon afterward.

After this confrontation, the more brutal whites fled the mission in fear, leaving behind only the few friendly ones, who were loved by the Indians. This moment of violence ended this particular reign of terror for the Pawnees, but the raids by their Indian neighbors continued unrelentingly.

In dire need, the Pawnees became infamous for their raids on the white travelers. Sometimes they would beg gifts from travelers on the Oregon Trail, who were heading for the Northwest. One young tough from the East vowed he would shoot the first Indian he saw. It was a young Pawnee woman.

HUNGER AND A DIRE SITUATION OFTEN FORCED THE PAWNEE
TO TURN TO RAIDING WAGON TRAINS AS THEY MOVED
ACROSS THE GREAT PLAINS TO THE WEST. THIS PAINTING,
"THE ATTACK ON AN EMIGRANT TRAIN" PAINTED BY CHARLES
WIMAR IN 1856, DEPICTS SUCH AN EVENT.

THIS PAINTING ON AN ANIMAL HIDE SHOWS A WARRING
INDIAN BAND ATTACKING A GROUP OF PAWNEE.

Enraged Pawnees descended on the wagon train, demanding the culprit. The other travelers had no wish to fight a large party of furious Indians, so they turned the killer over to the Pawnee warriors, and he was skinned from head to foot. A nearby stream is still known as Rawhide Creek.

The U.S. government forced the Pawnee to move to a new reservation, and by 1860, a grist mill, a saw mill, and other bounty of the white man had been provided. Things seemed to be looking up, at least materially, for the unfortunate tribe. But the Sioux, Arapaho, and Cheyenne would not let the Pawnee live in peace. The Pawnee appealed to the United States for protection, but it was never provided effectively.

The United States eventually decided to suppress these war-loving tribes, and asked the Pawnee chiefs to lend some warriors to the cause. The young Pawnee braves were eager, and this began their tradition of fighting with the U.S. Army, and even serving as guides.

By the 1870s, the Pawnee, still suffering from starvation and hounded by the Sioux, felt a desperate need to change their environment. They looked southward to the Indian Territory, in what is now Oklahoma. Reluctantly, in 1874, they moved there. It was a sad trek, for they were leaving their longtime

A DELEGATION OF PAWNEE CALLS ON PRESIDENT U.S. GRANT
AT THE WHITE HOUSE IN WASHINGTON, D.C.

THIS PAWNEE FAMILY POSES IN A TEPEE SHORTLY AFTER THE
PAWNEE REMOVAL FROM NEBRASKA IN THE 1880S.

U.S. PAWNEE SCOUTS IN 1869. THE SCOUTS WERE RECRUITED BY THE U.S. ARMY IN ITS STRUGGLE AGAINST OTHER INDIAN PEOPLES. THEY ALSO PROTECTED WORKERS AS THEY BUILT THE TRANSCONTINENTAL RAILROAD.

home in Nebraska. And it turned out to be no escape from the tribe's constant companions—misery and sickness.

But the Pawnee had one last moment of glory. Several bands of Sioux and Cheyenne had abandoned their reservations to the north and were preying on white settlements. The U.S. Army remembered the Pawnee Scouts and went to their new home to ask for one hundred men. Pawnee males, young and old, healthy and feeble, clamored to be chosen. When the army had picked its hundred men and they were departing by train for Kansas, crowds of young Pawnee braves followed the railroad cars for miles on foot, begging to be allowed to fight without pay.

The Pawnee Scouts, although outnumbered, served with distinction, routing several large bands of Sioux. Many herds of horses were presented to the Scouts by the Army in recognition of their bravery and service.

THE PAWNEE CONTINUE THEIR TRADITIONS
IN PAWNEE, OKLAHOMA.

THE PAWNEE TODAY

The Pawnee have made a distinct comeback in numbers and morale from their low point at the beginning of the century. For many years after their arrival in Indian Territory, their outlook was very depressed. Government representatives, who were supposed to help and guide the Indians, were often indifferent to them, sometimes to the point of actually cheating them. Many Indians, including Pawnees, just gave up and lived on government handouts, at a very low level. When Oklahoma became a state in 1907, the Pawnee were set adrift in a sea of whites. They had no tribe, only people.

But in the 1930s, the federal government seemed to awaken to the tragedy of the rootless Indians and helped the Pawnee to again become a functioning tribe. In the 1960s, the United States began to be more aware of the injustices that American Indians had suffered, and began to make attempts to right the past wrongs.

Today, the Pawnee number about 2,400 people. More than half of them live near the tribal headquarters in Pawnee, Oklahoma, about 100 miles (161 km)

PAWNEE TRIBAL HEADQUARTERS
IN PAWNEE, OKLAHOMA

PAWNEE, OKLAHOMA, IS HOME TO APPROXIMATELY
HALF OF TODAY'S TRIBAL POPULATION.

northeast of Oklahoma City. The remainder are scat-
tered throughout the southwest and California, many
living in cities. They are active in the industries of the
region, such as agriculture, oil, and cattle. Some work
at tribal headquarters, some at hospitals and the state
university. There is considerable intermarriage with
their former sworn enemies, the Cheyenne and Sioux.

DANCER RONALD GOODEAGLE AT A PAWNEE CEREMONY.

PAWNEE DANCE AND HERITAGE IS PASSED
FROM GENERATION TO GENERATION
AS IT HAS BEEN FOR CENTURIES.

Most of the Pawnee children go to public schools, although others go to private Indian schools. Ike Matthews, an official at the Pawnee headquarters, said, "Some like to go away to school because there is little to do in Pawnee."

There are active programs to fight alcoholism, Matthews said, as with other tribes. The drug prob-

IN CONTRAST TO THE NINETEENTH CENTURY, PAWNEE CHILDREN ARE TODAY TAUGHT THEIR OWN LANGUAGE IN THEIR OWN SCHOOLS.

GARLAND AND FRANCES KENT ARE PART OF A
HOPEFUL FUTURE FOR THE PAWNEE PEOPLE.

lem which had become serious, now seems to be lessening.

Most encouraging of all, he felt, is that many young Pawnee are beginning to study their own language, which had been on the way to becoming forgotten. In fact, a modern historian of the tribe, Carl N. Tyson, says, "Today the future appears bright for the Pawnee. They have a forceful leadership, and they are enjoying new freedoms."

GLOSSARY

Anthropologist   a scientist who studies the human race.

Buffalo   a large, ox-like animal (more correctly called the bison) once common in the western United States. It was hunted almost to extinction.

Cache   a place where things are kept, such as food.

Cholera   an often deadly disease that spreads among many people.

Community   a group of people, such as a village.

Democratic   a system under which each person has a right to follow his own wishes, so long as he does not interfere with the rights of others.

Dictatorial   a system under which a leader forces people to think and live in a certain way, without their having a choice.

Epidemic   an illness that spreads rapidly among many people.

Hut   a small dwelling. It is usually not moveable.

Lodge   a dwelling place.

Missionary   a person sent by churches to spread a religion and to do educational and charitable work.

Nomadic   traveling and living in many places.

Ritual   a set form in which a ceremony, religious or otherwise, is performed.

Rustlers   a slang expression for cattle or horse thieves.

Smallpox   a deadly, contagious disease.

Tipi (also spelled teepee)   a cone-shaped dwelling, made of the skins of animals or cloth wrapped around a wooden frame. It can be moved.

FOR FURTHER READING

Avery, Susan and Linda Skinner. *Extraordinary American Indians*. Chicago: Childrens Press, 1992.

Cohen, Carol L. *Mud Pony*. New York: Scholastic, Inc., 1989.

Fradin, Dennis B. *The Pawnee*. Chicago: Childrens Press, 1988.

Howell, War Cry. *Gramma Curlychief's Pawnee Indian Stories*. Los Altos, CA: Davenport, May Publishers, 1985.

Tyson, Carl N. *The Pawnee People*. Phoenix: Indian Tribal Series, 1976.

Weltfish, Gene. *The Lost Universe*. New York: Basic Books, 1965.

Williamson, Ray A. *Living in the Sky*. Boston: Houghton Mifflin, 1984.

INDEX

ABOUT THE AUTHOR

Arthur Myers has been a newspaper and magazine writer and editor and has published a number of books, several of them for children. He is author of another book in this series, *The Cheyenne*. He lives in Wellesley, Massachusetts.